THE LIBRARY
PIANO
CLASSICS

COMPILED BY AMY APPLEBY AND PETER PICKOW

WITH SPECIAL THANKS TO ZORAYA MENDEZ-DE COSMIS FOR HER INVALUABLE GUIDANCE IN THE PREPARATION OF THIS VOLUME.

ORDER NO. AM 91728
US INTERNATIONAL STANDARD BOOK NUMBER: 0.8256.1377.9
UK INTERNATIONAL STANDARD BOOK NUMBER: 0.7119.3844.X

EXCLUSIVE DISTRIBUTORS:
MUSIC SALES CORPORATION
257 PARK AVENUE SOUTH, NEW YORK, NY 10010 USA
MUSIC SALES LIMITED
8/9 FRITH STREET, LONDON W1V 5TZ ENGLAND
MUSIC SALES PTY. LIMITED
120 ROTHSCHILD STREET, ROSEBERY, SYDNEY, NSW 2018, AUSTRALIA

PRINTED IN THE UNITED STATES OF AMERICA BY
VICKS LITHOGRAPH AND PRINTING CORPORATION

AMSCO PUBLICATIONS
NEW YORK/LONDON/SYDNEY

CONTENTS

Solfeggio

Carl Phillipp Emanuel Bach
(1714–1788)

Prelude No. 2

(from *Twelve Little Preludes*)

Johann Sebastian Bach
(1685–1750)

Gavotte II: La Musette

(from *English Suite No. 6*)

Johann Sebastian Bach
(1685–1750)

Sarabande

(from *French Suite No. 1*)

Johann Sebastian Bach
(1685–1750)

Gavotte

(from *French Suite No. 5*)

Johann Sebastian Bach
(1685–1750)

Two-Part Invention No. 1

Johann Sebastian Bach
(1685–1750)

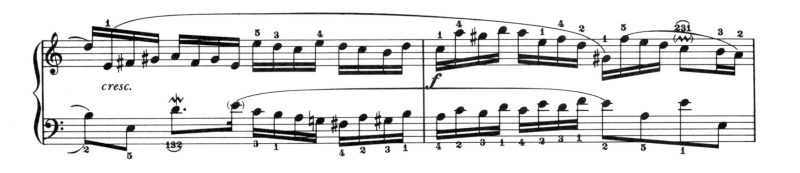

Two-Part Invention No. 4

Johann Sebastian Bach
(1685–1750)

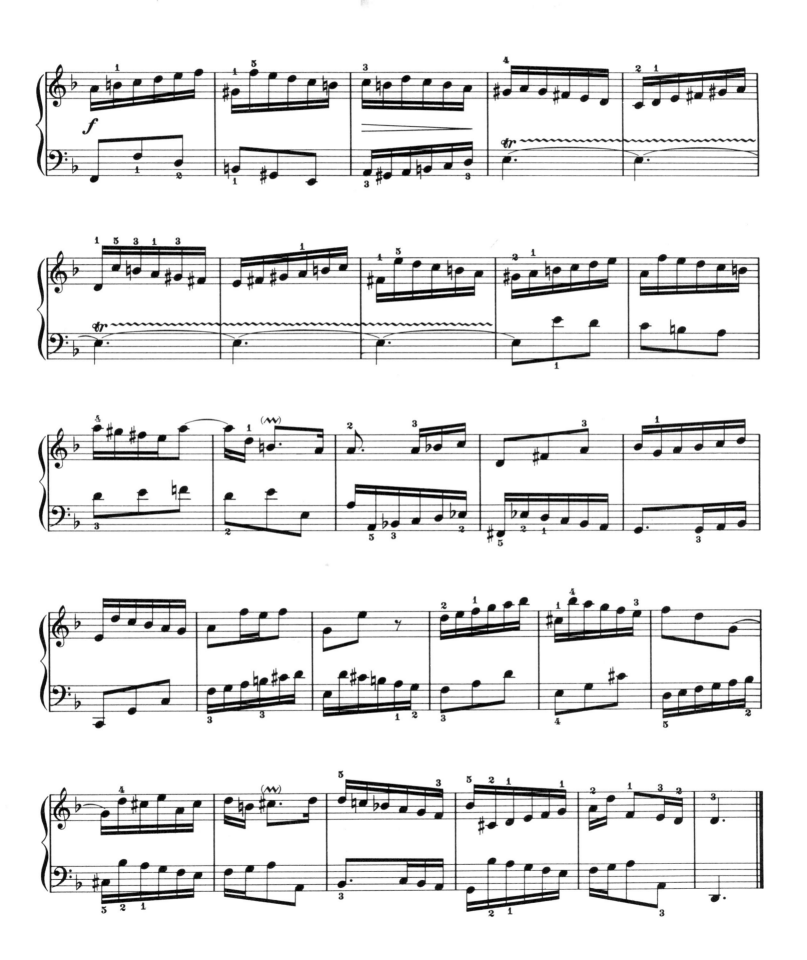

Two-Part Invention No. 8

Johann Sebastian Bach
(1685–1750)

Two-Part Invention No. 14

Johann Sebastian Bach
(1685–1750)

Allegretto

Three-Part Invention No. 9

Johann Sebastian Bach
(1685–1750)

Prelude and Fugue No. 7

(from *The Well-Tempered Clavier, Book I*)

Johann Sebastian Bach
(1685–1750)

Prelude

24

Fugue

25

Three Little Pieces

Béla Bartók
(1881–1945)

Allegro robusto.

III

leggiero il basso

simile

Andante

(from *Symphony No. 1*)

Ludwig van Beethoven
(1770–1827)

Allegretto

(from *Symphony No. 7*)

Ludwig van Beethoven
(1770–1827)

Turkish March

(from *The Ruins of Athens*)

Ludwig van Beethoven
(1770–1827)

Sonatina No. 1 in G Major

Ludwig van Beethoven
(1770–1827)

Romanza

Allegretto (♩. = 76)

Sonatina No. 2 in F Major

Ludwig van Beethoven
(1770–1827)

Allegro assai

40

Rondo.
Allegro.

Sonata Pathétique

(Op. 13)

Ludwig van Beethoven
(1770–1827)

Allegro di molto e con brio

Allegro molto e con brio

Adagio cantabile

52

Rondo
Allegro

Intermezzo

(Op. 118, No. 2)

Johannes Brahms
(1833–1897)

Andante teneramente

Waltz in E Major

Op. 39, No. 2

Johannes Brahms
(1833–1897)

Waltz in B♭ Major

(Op. 39, No. 8)

Johannes Brahms
(1833–1897)

Hungarian Dance No. 7

Johannes Brahms
(1833–1897)

Ballade

(after the Scottish Ballad "Edward," Op. 10, No. 1)

Johannes Brahms
(1833–1897)

Allegro, ma non troppo

Prelude in E Minor

(Op. 28, No. 4)

Frédéric Chopin
(1810–1849)

Prelude in C Minor

(Op. 28, No. 20)

Frédéric Chopin
(1810–1849)

Largo

Prelude in B♭ Major

(Op. 28, No. 21)

Frédéric Chopin
(1810–1849)

Cantabile

Raindrop Prelude

(Op. 28, No. 15)

Frédéric Chopin
(1810–1849)

76

Waltz in A♭ Major

(Op. 69, No. 1, Posthumous)

Frédéric Chopin
(1810–1849)

Waltz in E♭ Major

(Op. 18)

Frédéric Chopin
(1810–1849)

Mazurka in C Major

(Op. 67, No. 3)

Frédéric Chopin
(1810–1849)

Nocturne in D♭ Major

(Op. 27, No. 2)

Frédéric Chopin
(1810–1849)

Lento sostenuto (♩. = 50.)

Polonaise Militaire

(Op. 40, No. 1)

Frédéric Chopin
(1810–1849)

Allegro con brio

Funeral March

(from *Sonata*, Op. 35, No. 2)

Frédéric Chopin
(1810–1849)

Rêverie

Claude Debussy
(1862–1918)

Le Petit-Rien

François Couperin
(1668–1733)

109

The Little Shepherd

(from *Children's Corner*)

Claude Debussy
(1862–1918)

The Maid with the Flaxen Hair

(La fille aux cheveux de lin)

Claude Debussy
(1862–1918)

Sarabande

(from *Pour le piano*)

Claude Debussy
(1862–1918)

115

Pizzicati

(from *Sylvia*)

Léo Delibes
(1836–1891)

Largo

(from *New World Symphony*)

Antonín Dvořák
(1841–1904)

121

Silhouette

(Op. 8, No. 2)

Antonín Dvořák
(1841–1904)

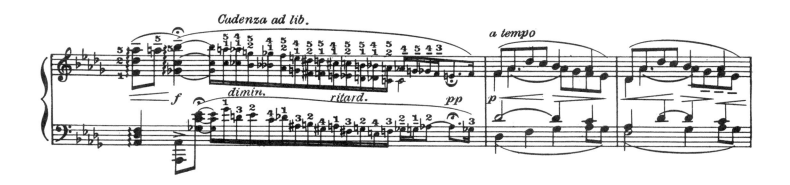

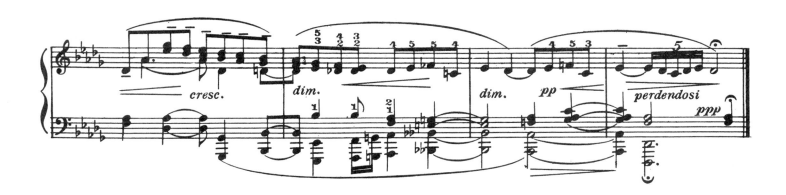

Berceuse

(from *Jocelyn*)

Benjamin Godard
(1849–1895)

Andante

(from *Orpheus*)

Christoph Willibald von Gluck
(1714–1787)

The Dying Poet

(Meditation)

Louis Moreau Gottschalk
(1829–1869)

128

130

Morning

(from *Peer Gynt*)

Edvard Grieg
(1843–1907)

To Spring

(Op. 43, No. 5)

Edvard Grieg
(1843–1907)

Passacaille

George Frideric Handel
(1685–1759)

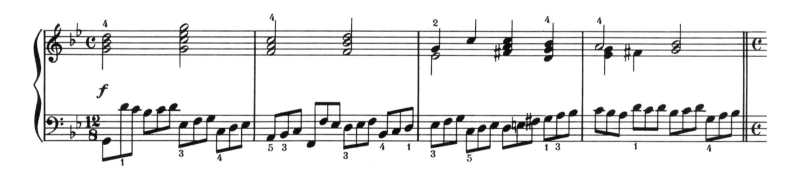

Sarabande

George Frideric Handel
(1685–1759)

Andante

(from *Surprise Symphony*)

Franz Joseph Haydn
(1732–1809)

Andante Grazioso

Franz Joseph Haydn
(1732–1809)

Allegro in F Major

Franz Joseph Haydn
(1732–1809)

Minuetto Giocoso

Franz Joseph Haydn
(1732–1809)

Trio.

I. volta *mf*
II. volta *p*

marcato

brillante

D. C. al Fine.

An Alexis

Johann Nepomuk Hummel
(1778–1837)

Andantino espressivo

The Danube Waves

Iosif Ivanovici
(1845–1902)

Introduction
Allegro moderato

Coda

D.S. al Fine

The Entertainer

Scott Joplin
(1868–1917)

159

D. S. al Coda ⊕ CODA

Flower Song

(Op. 39)

Gustav Lange
(1830–1889)

164

Waltz

(from *The Merry Widow*)

Franz Lehár
(1870–1948)

Tempo di Valse *Molto e tranquillo*

Consolation No. 5

Franz Liszt
(1811–1886)

169

Wedding March

(from *A Midsummer Night's Dream*)

Felix Mendelssohn
(1809–1847)

Nocturne

(from *A Midsummer Night's Dream*)

Felix Mendelssohn
(1809–1847)

Little Piece

(Op. 72, No. 1)

Felix Mendelssohn
(1809–1847)

Allegro non troppo.

Spring Song
(Op. 62, No. 6)

Felix Mendelssohn
(1809–1847)

Allegretto grazioso

Consolation

Felix Mendelssohn
(1809–1847)

Adagio non troppo

Confidence

(Op. 19, No. 4)

Felix Mendelssohn
(1809–1847)

Venetian Boat Song No. 2

(Op. 30, No. 6)

Felix Mendelssohn
(1809–1847)

Capriccio in A Major

(Op. 16, No. 1)

Felix Mendelssohn
(1809–1847)

Andante con moto

183

184

185

Minuet No. 1

Wolfgang Amadeus Mozart
(1756–1791)

Minuetto da Capo al Fine

12 Variations

(K. 265, *Ah! vous dirai-je, maman*)

Wolfgang Amadeus Mozart
(1756–1791)

Theme

VAR. VI

VAR. VII

VAR. VIII
Minore

VAR. IX
Maggiore

194

Minuet

(from *Don Juan*)

Wolfgang Amadeus Mozart
(1756–1791)

Sonata in A Major

(K. 331)

Wolfgang Amadeus Mozart
(1756–1791)

198

Var. II.

Var. III.
Minore.

200

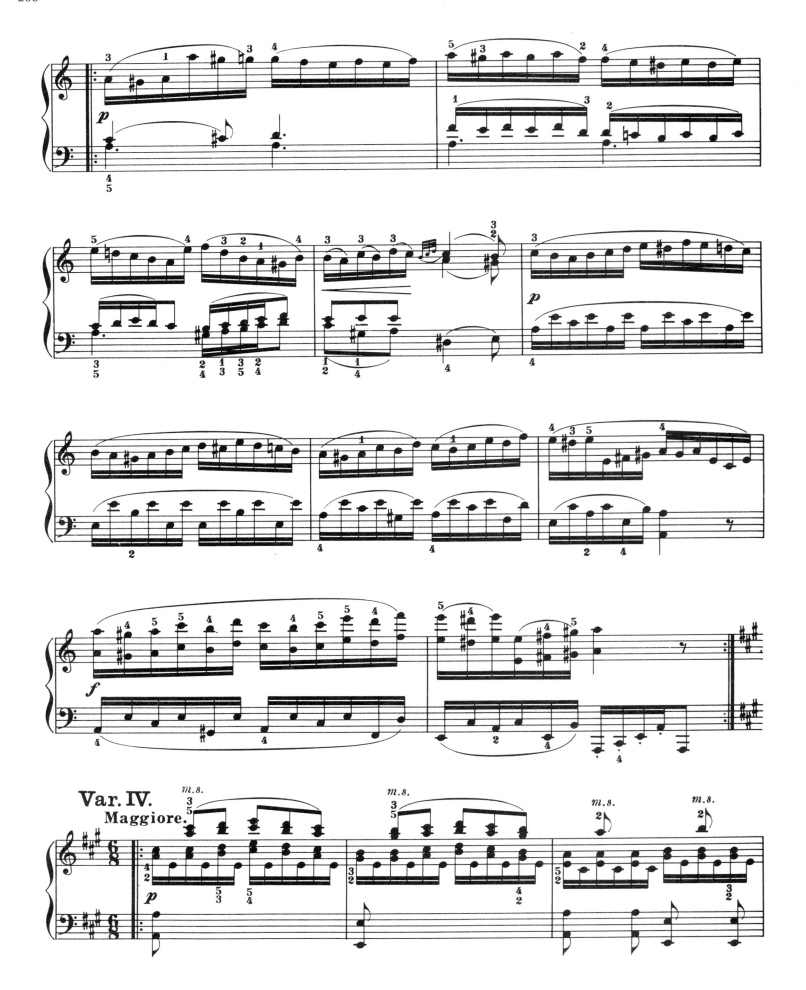

Var. V.
Adagio.

Var. VI.
Allegro.

205

(*Menuetto D.C.*)

208

Alla Turca.
Allegretto.

Narcissus

(Op. 13, No. 4)

Ethelbert Nevin
(1862–1901)

Andante con moto

Can-Can

(from *Orpheus in the Underworld*)

Jacques Offenbach
(1819–1880)

Dance of the Hours

(from *La Gioconda*)

Amilcare Ponchielli
(1834–1886)

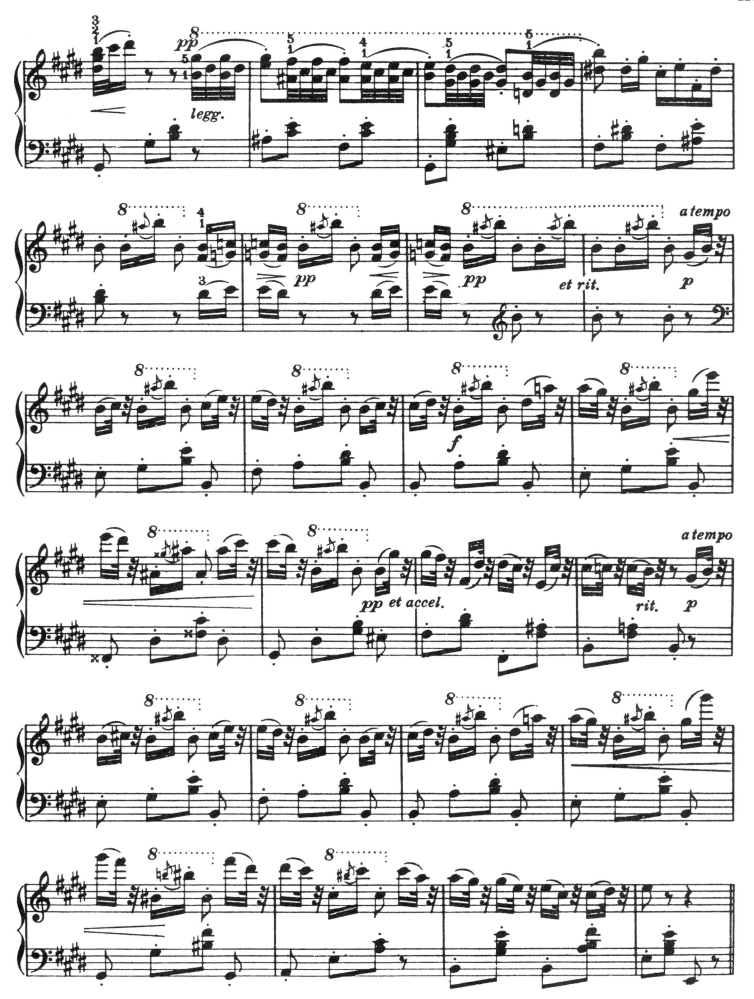

March

(from *Love for Three Oranges*)

Sergei Prokofiev
(1891–1953)

Tempo di Marcia

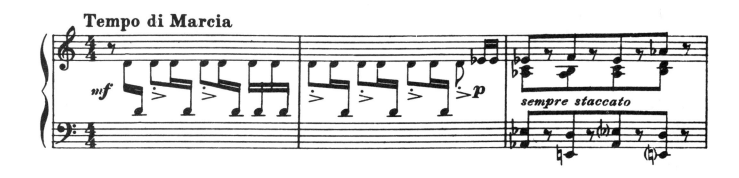

Minuet in A Minor

Henry Purcell
(1659–1695)

Prelude in G Minor

(Op. 23, No. 5)

Sergei Rachmaninoff
(1873–1943)

Poco meno mosso

poco a poco accelerando e cresc. al tempo primo

232

Piano Concerto No. 2

(themes)

Sergei Rachmaninoff
(1873–1943)

Moderato

(2nd Theme)
Moderately slow

The Young Prince and the Young Princess

(from *Scheherezade*)

Nikolai Rimsky-Korsakov
(1844—1908)

Andantino, quasi allegretto M.M. ♩.= 54

Melody in F

(Op. 3, No. 1)

Anton Rubinstein
(1829–1894)

239

240

Romance

(Op. 44, No. 1)

Anton Rubinstein
(1829–1894)

The Swan

(from *Carnival of the Animals*)

Camille Saint-Saëns
(1835–1921)

246

Sonata in C Major

(Kp 159)

Domenico Scarlatti
(1685–1757)

Allegro

Trois Gymnopédies

Erik Satie
(1866—1925)

1

252

2

3

Pastorale

Domenico Scarlatti
(1685–1757)

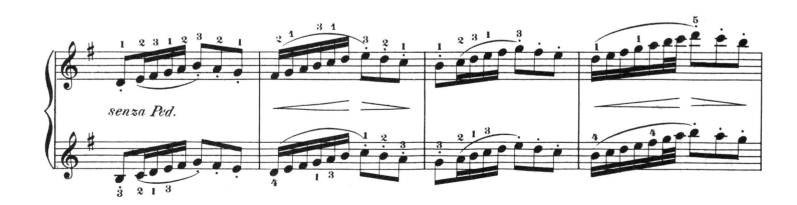

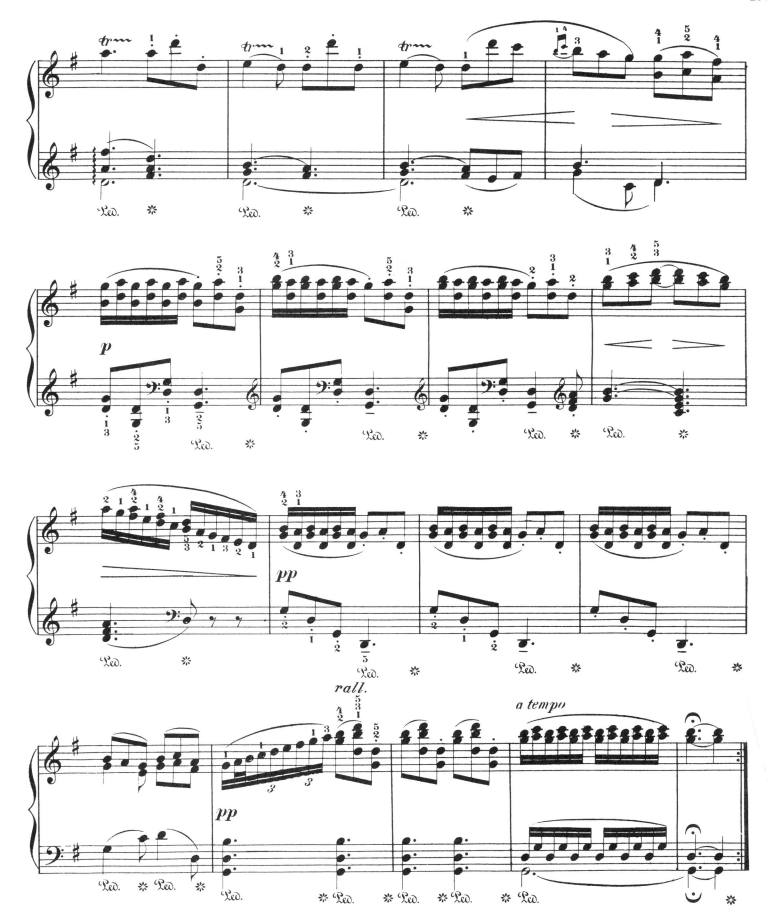

Ave Maria

Franz Schubert
(1797–1828)

Andante

(from *Impromptu,* Op. 142, No. 3)

Franz Schubert
(1797–1828)

Entr'acte

(from *Rosamunde*)

Franz Schubert
(1797–1828)

Scherzo in B♭ Major

Franz Schubert
(1797–1828)

Allegretto

Walzer

Franz Schubert
(1797–1828)

268

270

Why?

(Warum?, Op. 12, No. 3)

Robert Schumann
(1810–1856)

Langsam und zart
(Lento e teneramente)

Romance

(from *Album for the Young*)

Robert Schumann
(1810–1856)

Knight Rupert

(from *Album for the Young*)

Robert Schumann
(1810—1856)

276

Rustle of Spring

(Op. 32, No. 1)

Christian Sinding
(1856–1941)

Agitato

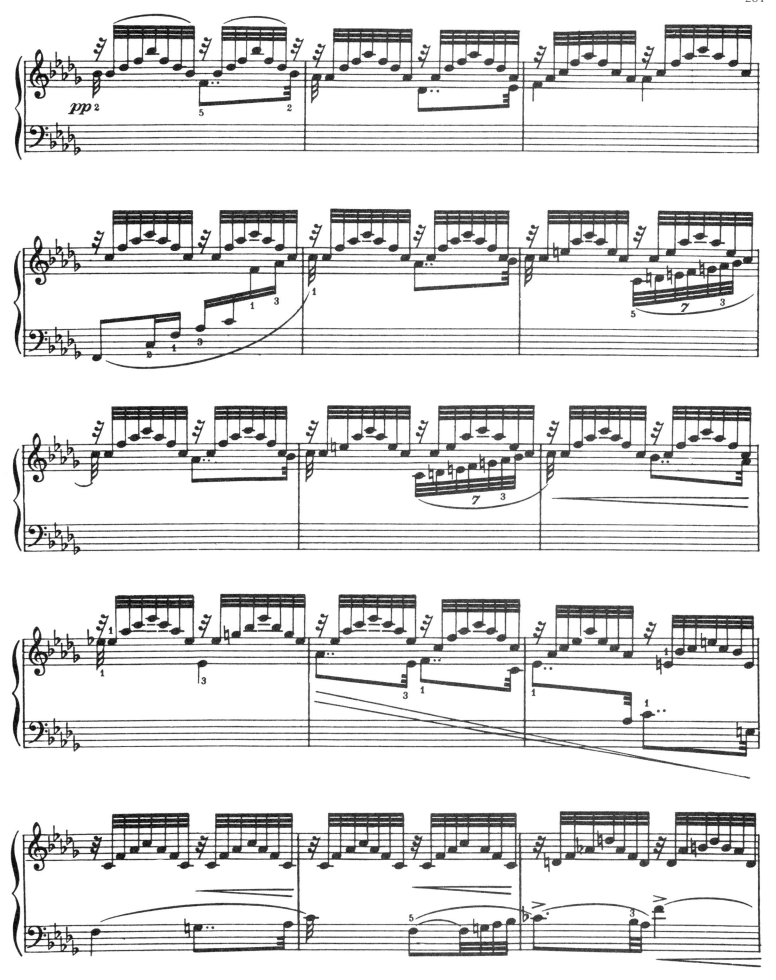

Finlandia

Jan Sibelius
(1865–1957)

Moderately bright *(slow two beats)*

Tales from the Vienna Woods

Johann Strauss
(1825–1899)

Dance of the Sugar Plum Fairy

(from *The Nutcracker*)

Peter Ilyich Tchaikovsky
(1840–1893)

298

Waltz of the Flowers

(from *The Nutcracker*)

Peter Ilyich Tchaikovsky
(1840–1893)

300

302

June

(Barcarolle)

Peter Ilyich Tchaikovsky
(1840–1893)

Andante cantabile
Tempo I

Bridal Chorus

(from *Lohengrin*)

Richard Wagner
(1813–1883)

312

The Skaters Waltz

(*Les Patineurs*)

Emil Waldteufel
(1837–1915)

Theme and Variation

(Op. 7, *Vien qua Dorina bella*)

Carl Maria von Weber
(1786–1826)

Tema.

Andante con espressione.

Var.
Sempre dolce legato.

The Dove

(La Paloma)

Sebastian Yradier
(1809–1865)